Our Class Traits

Gathering Data

Marisa Pace

COMPUTER SCIENCE For the REAL World™

Rosen Classroom™

Published in 2018 by The Rosen Publishing Group, Inc.
29 East 21st Street, New York, NY 10010

Book Design: Jennifer Ryder-Talbot
Editor: Caitie McAneney

Photo Credits: Cover, p. 4, 6, 10, 12 Monkey Business Images/Shutterstock.com; p. 8 Littlekidmoment/Shutterstock.com.

ISBN: 9781538351888
6-pack ISBN: 9781508136651

Manufactured in the United States of America

CPSIA Compliance Information: Batch #WS18RC: For Further Information contact Rosen Publishing, New York, New York at 1-800-237-9932

Table of Contents

Learning About Genes

We are learning about **genes** in science class. Genes are passed down from parents to their children. They control **traits**, including how each person looks. Miss Garcia gives us a project. We have to gather **data** on the traits in our class.

Looking at Traits

You can see many kinds of physical traits, such as skin color. What kinds of traits can we gather data about? We decide to look at hair color, eye color, and height. We gather data by passing out a sheet with questions. Each person fills out a sheet about hair and eye color.

eye color | #
blue | 4
green | 2
brown | 10

Eye Data

Miss Garcia gathers the sheets. We take turns writing the data on the board. Under eye color, we write three options: blue, green, and brown. Four kids have blue eyes. Two kids have green eyes. Ten kids have brown eyes.

U GET

Hair Data

There are three options for hair color: brown, black, and yellow. Miss Garcia says yellow hair is also called blond. Eight kids have brown hair. Four kids have black hair. Four kids have blond hair. Brown hair is the most common.

hair color	#
brown	8
black	4
yellow	4

Height Data

The last trait we look at is height. Miss Garcia measures everyone with a yardstick. She puts kids into groups by height: tall, medium, or short. Five kids are tall. Eight kids are medium height. Three kids are short.

height	#
tall	5
medium	8
short	3

Let's Brainstorm!

"How else could we gather data?" Miss Garcia asks. We brainstorm new ways. We could count raised hands. We could make an online quiz that gathers answers. There are many ways to gather and order data about our class traits!

Glossary

data: Information often written as numbers; facts about something.

gene: A part of a cell that controls how a living thing looks or grows.

trait: Something that makes one person or thing different from another.

Index